DINOSAURS, DRAGONFLIES & DIAMONDS

ALL ABOUT NATURAL HISTORY MUSEUMS

DINOSAURS, DRAGONFLIES & DIAMONDS

ALL ABOUT NATURAL HISTORY MUSEUMS

BY GAIL GIBBONS

FOUR WINDS PRESS   NEW YORK

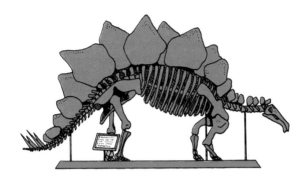

Special thanks to Steve Quinn, Mel Alburger, Naomi Weintstein, and Penelope Boudrie-Sanders of the American Museum of Natural History, New York, New York.

Four Winds Press, Macmillan Publishing Company, 866 Third Avenue, New York, NY 10022. Collier Macmillan Canada, Inc.
First Edition   Printed in the United States of America

10   9   8   7   6   5   4   3   2   1

The text of this book is set in 16 point Raleigh. The illustrations are rendered in pen-and-ink by the artist with color preseparated by Post Graphics.

Library of Congress Cataloging-in-Publication Data
Gibbons, Gail.   Dinosaurs, dragonflies & diamonds: all about natural history museums/by Gail Gibbons.—1st ed.   p. cm. Summary: Describes what one may find in a natural history museum and the work that goes on behind the scenes.
ISBN 0-02-737240-5
1. Natural history museums—Juvenile literature. [1. Natural history museums.] I. Title. II. Title: Dinosaurs, dragonflies, and diamonds.   QH70.A1G53 1988   508'.074—dc 19   88-388 CIP   AC

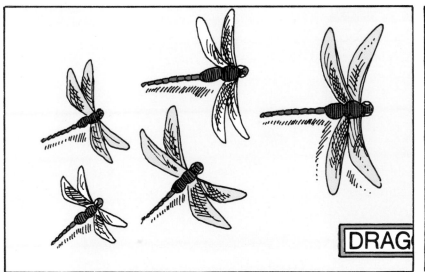

DRAG

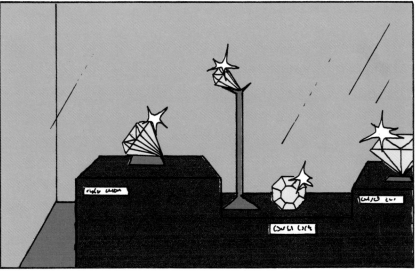

Millions of dinosaur bones, big and small dragonflies, glittering diamonds under one roof! Natural history museums have many exhibits to look at and huge collections of stored objects to study. Their subject: the history of nature and human beings.

The first natural history museum in the United States was formed in 1773 in South Carolina. The people of that state were expected to provide the collections. They were asked to give "...the various fossils, minerals and ores, the different soils, clays, marles, stones, sands and shells...."

There are now many natural history museums in the United States, and in the rest of the world as well. Some are small.

Others are huge.

Visitors from all over the world come to the museums.
There is much to see.

There are exhibits of birds...plants...

fishes ...

and wild animals. Some of the exhibits are called habitat groups.
They show the way the animals look in their natural homes.

There are displays about the history of human beings...

about gems … about bugs … and more.

Dinosaurs! They lived millions of years ago. Visitors stare up at the huge standing skeletons.

Most of the exhibits at natural history museums are there all the time. They are called permanent exhibits.

But often there are special shows. They are called temporary exhibits. GOLD! Banners advertise the special event. Gold nuggets shine in their display cases.

A movie about the California gold rush appears on the screen in the background. Look! A gold bar and lots of gold jewelry. Gold everywhere!

A group of visitors listen to their tour guide. "This pottery is about four thousand years old." Another tour group of school-children is close behind.

Natural history museums often have gift shops. Some visitors buy books. Others buy souvenirs to remind them of their visit.

Throughout the year, the museums present special lectures and activities for visitors to attend. Some people sign up for trips with museum tour guides. Often the trips are to faraway places.

Scientists come to natural history museums to study the vast collections. Behind closed doors, they take their notes. They find drawers and drawers of stones... animal bones...

Indian clothing ... beetles....

Millions and millions of objects are stored here.

Behind the scenes, it takes many workers for the museums to run smoothly. Some workers are busy labeling, tagging, and recording all of the many stored items.

Staff scientists work in their labs, making new discoveries about nature and people.

How a New Rattlesnake Exhibit Is Made

The museum sends a curator—the person in charge of the exhibit—and artists on an expedition.

curator

background artist

The background artist paints what the location looks like.

foreground artist

The foreground artist collects plants, rocks, and sand.

Museums often create new exhibits, too.

A zoo has donated several dead rattlesnakes to the museum. The sculptor will make plastic snakes for the exhibit.

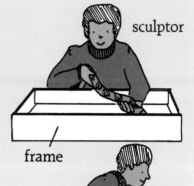

sculptor

frame

1. First, a snake is pinned in position.

2. Rubber is poured into the frame.

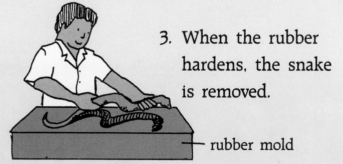

3. When the rubber hardens, the snake is removed.

rubber mold

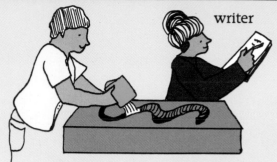

writer

4. Then, liquid plastic is poured into the mold.

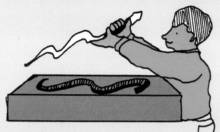

5. When the plastic hardens, the exhibit snake is removed.

6. When all three plastic snakes are ready, they are carefully painted.

The background is painted.

The rattlesnakes look alive in their natural setting.

papier-mâché rock

Everything is put in place.

The plants here are not real. They were made to look like plants brought back to the museum.

Other workers handle museum business. Many are there to assist visitors and answer their questions.

Natural history museums are where to go to have fun, to make new discoveries...and to see the dinosaurs!